This book belongs to:

CORONAVIRUS
A BOOK FOR KIDS

Written and Illustrated
By R.L. Margolin

J. EMMETT PRESS

For Lavie, Hadassah, and Jack:

There was a time we couldn't go home and now we must stay home. Whatever comes our way, we are home when we are together.

With heartfelt gratitude to those in the trenches:

Thank you for your courage and sacrifice.

ISBN 978-1-0878-7748-1

Text copyright © 2020 by Rachel Miller.
Illustrations copyright © 2020 by Rachel Miller.
All rights reserved. Published by the J. Emmett Press
Bronx, New York.

The illustrations in this book are created using digital collage of hand drawn art, rendered in colored pencil and ink.

Hey Grown-ups,

Do the children in your life have questions about the new coronavirus, COVID-19? Children feel secure when adults listen to their feelings and answer their questions honestly, with age appropriate detail. Sometimes the honest answer might be "I don't know," or "I'll see if I can find out," too! I hope this book is helpful for you in starting a conversation with your children about our new normal.

Sending Strength,

R.L. Margolin

Coronavirus Pandemic Glossary

Even as adults, we are just learning the detailed meaning of some terms that have suddenly become part of our everyday vocabulary. It is easier to explain situations to our kids when we have a clear understanding ourselves. Below are the official definitions of some words that are part of our new normal.

Social Distancing- Deliberately increasing the physical space between people to avoid spreading illness. This can include canceling events that will draw crowds, working or going to school from home, and trying to stay six feet away from people you don't live with. *

Quarantine- People who have been exposed to the new coronavirus and are at risk for coming down with COVID-19 spend two weeks staying home with no visitors, using strict hygiene, and staying six feet away from everyone, including the people they live with.*

Isolation- People who are confirmed to have COVID-19 stay physically away from those who are not sick. This can take place in a hospital, or at home. Healthy people don't enter the sick person's room without protective equipment.*

Lockdown/Shelter In Place- A local government order to stay home to avoid the spread of COVID-19. The details of the restrictions on leaving your home depend on what your local government has decided. Sometimes the order is about the same as social distancing, if necessary there could be greater restrictions to the times a person can leave the house and what activities are allowed. **

* Physical Distancing and Self-Quarantine, Reviewed dby Lisa Lockerd Maragakis, M.D., M.P.H, www.hopkinsmedicine.org
** Governor Gavin Newsom Issues Stay at Home Order, Office of Governor Gavin Newsom, March 19, 2020 www.gov.ca.gov/2020/03/19/governor-gavin-newsom-issues-stay-at-home-order/

So what is the coronavirus? You have probably heard about germs. Coronavirus is a kind of germ.

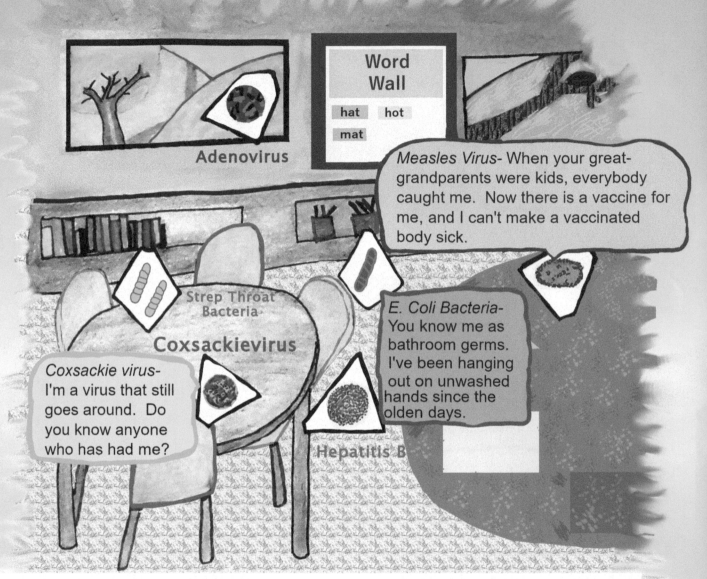

Germs are everywhere! People have been living in a world full of germs for a long, long time.

The white blood cells in our bodies are ready to handle many kinds of germs, and we have medicine to help people with many illnesses. Coronavirus is a new germ, so doctors are just learning how to help people who catch it. We want to slow the spread of this new germ to give doctors and scientists time to find a cure.

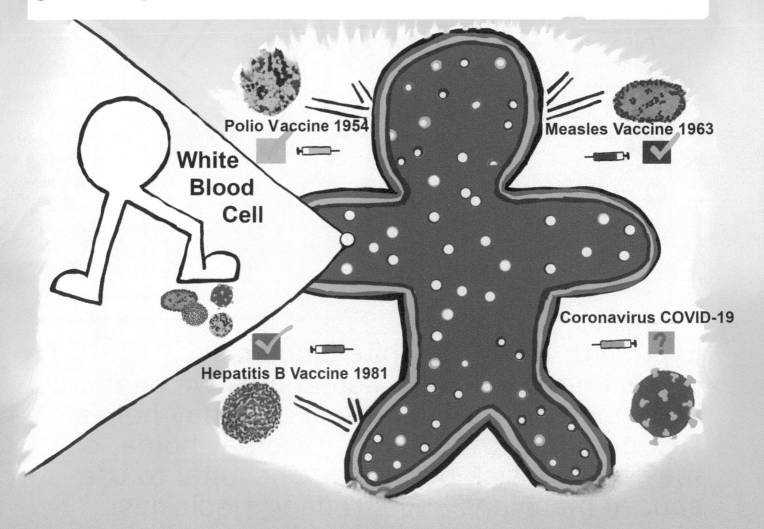

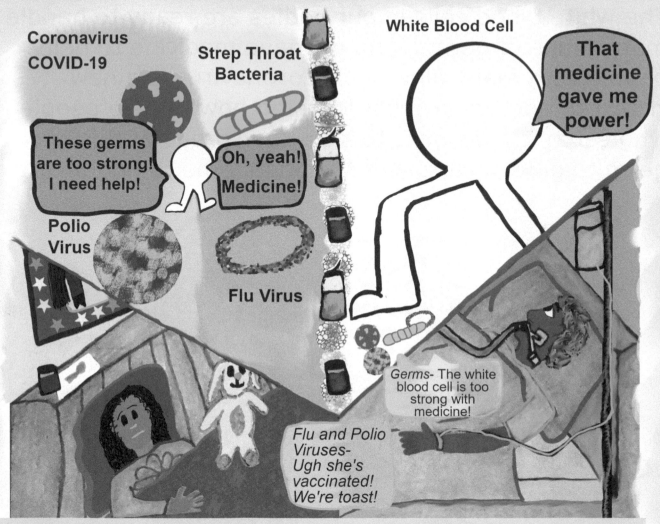

Even with all those white blood cells protecting our bodies, sometimes we need help handling germs. The doctor may help a sick person with medicine taken at home, or may bring a sick person to a hospital to use special machines and stronger medicines.

If you find out you've been near someone sick with coronavirus, you might need to stay home in quarantine for about two weeks. This helps stop the spread of germs.

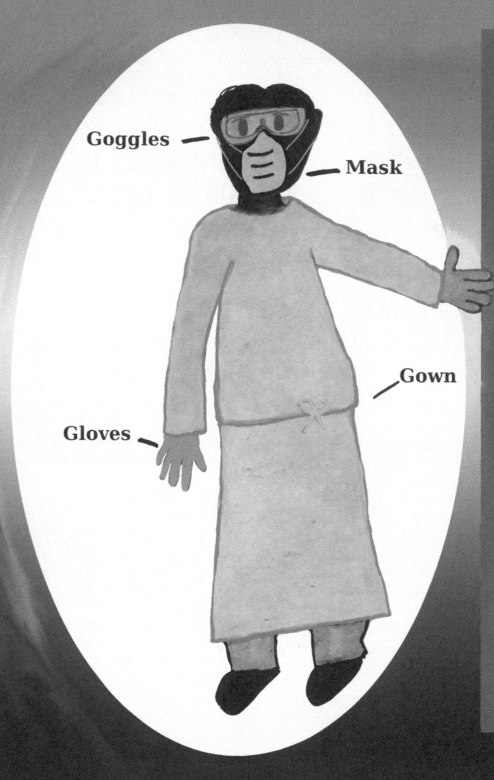

Goggles

Mask

Gown

Gloves

Some people who get sick with the new coronavirus will need to go to the hospital to get the right kind of help. Doctors and nurses in the hospital wear special suits so they don't get sick, or spread germs.

Most people who get sick from a virus get better. Some people become very sick from a virus, and die. Doctors and nurses work hard to help sick people. When a person feels sick, it is important to call a doctor for advice.

There are many things we can do to stay healthy, even when viruses are going around. One healthy habit is washing your hands, with soap.

Everyone coughs and sneezes. A healthy habit for handling coughing and sneezing is to cover your mouth and nose with your elbow when you feel that tickle. Better yet, cough or sneeze into a tissue. Then go wash your hands.

If you feel sick, tell a grown up. Sick people need to rest at home to get better. Staying home when you feel sick avoids spreading germs to your friends too!
Let's go home.
My head hurts.
Coronavirus- I was hoping to meet all the kids at school! I can't hop around making people sick if sick folks rest at home.

Your community may decide to to close crowded places for a while. This is another way to avoid spreading coronavirus.

Play Practice Canc

Carver Elementary Closed

Online school starts on Monday. Details on the way

shelter in place

Two week shelter in has been announced governor of Sealio

Tips for Online School

- Dress for school before you sign in.
- Have your books, a pencil, eraser, and paper nearby.
- Sit at a table or desk.
- Take your pets out of your room if they might distract you.

Capoeira Center

We will be movi online. Watch y details on signir

Central V

You might have seen people wearing masks like the one a doctor wears. People wear masks for many reasons, and not everyone who wears a mask is sick with coronavirus. In some communities, everyone is wearing a mask or a scarf outside the home, for now, to help stop coronavirus from spreading.

I'm feeling nervous about germs right now.

My doctor told me to wear this mask. I take a medicine that makes it hard for my body to handle germs.

I feel sick, and the doctor said I should come in for a checkup. I don't want to spread germs to other people waiting to see the doctor.

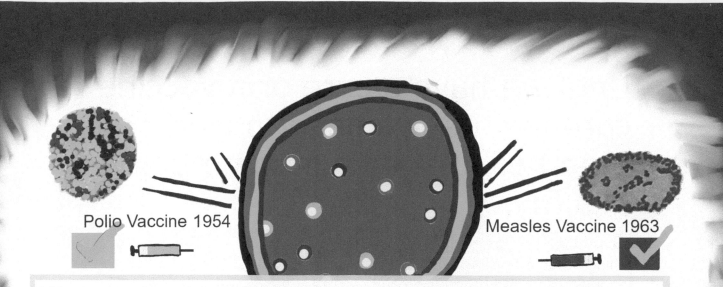

Polio Vaccine 1954

Measles Vaccine 1963

We now have vaccines to protect us from viruses that made many people sick in the old days. We don't have a vaccine for the new coronavirus, yet. Right now, all over the world, scientists are studying the coronavirus to try to find a cure for people who are sick, or a vaccine to protect us from catching it.

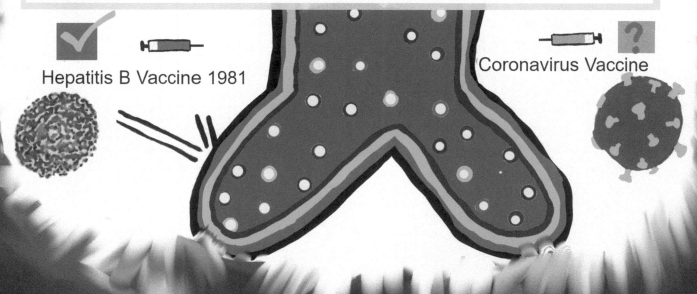

Hepatitis B Vaccine 1981

Coronavirus Vaccine

Until we have a cure or a vaccine for coronavirus, we need to work together to keep our community healthy.
Good hand washing takes 20 seconds. You can sing the "ABC" song to time yourself.
Health Tips
1. Stay home if you feel sick, and tell a grown up how you feel.
2. Wash your hands with soap often, especially when you come in from outside and before you eat. If you aren't near a sink, use hand sanitizer.
3. Cough or sneeze into your elbow, not your hand. Then go wash your hands.
4. Try to avoid touching your face.
5. Practice social distancing. Touch only people you live with, and give everyone else a six foot personal space bubble.
I don't feel good. I'm staying home.
Coronavirus- Hygiene mistakes let me jump to your friends.

You or your family might be asked to practice social distancing, to quarantine, or to stay in isolation to avoid spreading coronavirus. While our routines may change because of coronavirus, these changes are only for a time. The season of this new coronavirus, like all seasons, will pass.

There are many ways to stay in touch with your friends and family when visits are put on pause because of the coronavirus.

Even when we are alone in our homes, in our hearts we are in this together.
Every night at 7:00 pm we all go out on our balconies to cheer for the healthcare workers.

Do you have any questions? Do you have any feelings you'd like to share?

Sources

A note on viruses and bacteria in this book: Under a microscope, color varies depending on the stains used. Also, common names most families are familiar with are used to identify germs, even though those names are imprecise.

Ecoli- Symptoms of Intestinal Infection Due to E. Coli www.healthline.com/health/e-coli-infection

Hepatitis-B- Hepatitis B Questions and Answers for the Public www.cdc.gov/hepatitis/hbv/bfaq.htm

COVID-19/Coronavirus- Ocean County Department of Education Newsroom www.newsroom.ocde.us/coronavirus-update

Measles- Measles Virus Under Microscope www.cdc.gov/measles/symptoms/photos.htm

Strep Throat (streptococcus pyogenes)- Scientists find new variant of streptococcal bacteria causing sever infections by Sam Wong www.imperial.ac.uk/news/166651/scientists-find-variant-streptococcal-bacteria-causing/

Polio- Protein Databank in Europe, Bringing Structure to Biology, Poliovirus www.ebi.ac.uk/pdbe/entry/search/

Protective Equipment: COVID-19 PPE for Healthcare Professionals, by CDC, www.local768.org/wp-content/uploads/2020/COVID-19.jpg

General Information:
NYS On Pause www.coronavirus.health.ny.gov/new-york-state-pause
Governor Gavin Newsom Issues Stay at Home Order, Published Mar. 19, 2020 www.ca.gov

Lightning Source UK Ltd.
Milton Keynes UK
UKHW052152210620
365337UK00005B/24

9 781087 877471